COLLECTED
POEMS

By the same author
under her maiden name of Philippa Bunting
Frames of Mind
Heights of Folly
Courting Trouble
The Disenchanted Circle

Children's stories under her married name of Philippa Campbell
Higammy's Hovel
Back-to-Front Bunny
Honey and Crumpet
Kiki's Story
Minna and the Blackbird
Back of Beyond
Doctor Fovargue

ISBN 9780993349355

The Pine Marten Press
First published in 2021

Design by GSB (Edinburgh)

Philippa Campbell

COLLECTED
POEMS

Edited
with a Postscript by
David Campbell

CONTENTS

EXISTENTIAL ANGST

MAGICALLY COMPATIBLE

IN HARNESS

FOUR CHILDREN

THE SENIOR CITIZEN

HER MOTHER'S DAUGHTER

TIM

MEN

EARLY AND OCCASIONAL PIECES

EXISTENTIAL ANGST

TEMPTATION

Drowning, drowning in a surge of blood!
Unspirited, unsouled, while all this crimson flood
embraces flesh and earth, and cold disdain
sinks shivering.

And each aesthetic thought a wheel
that spins confusion each time I appeal
or question you.

Conflict, conflict of the warm and chill,
the animal with soul, the flesh with will,
and incoherent still.
Yet oh, how sweet
to swim and ride the flood!

Only think with me that passions should be curbed.
Just know me first and love first what I am.
You pledge respect for me as though to dam
the streams of niggling doubt the flood disturbed.

You ask me not to analyse desire;
for natural passion is itself entire
to justify desire, that hand in glove
we are together, moral in our love.

But as my liking for you grows, it burns
an acid discontent within my breast.
Soon, soon let fervour flare, then lie at rest,
or with conviction love convincingly
and, flesh and spirit, fling me to the sea!

I HAVE ENTERED EARTH ANEW

What use in anything I do
if I'm cast away from you?
What joy in paddock, stream or wood,
what use in virtue or in good,
what blessing in my being true
if it wrenches me from you?

I have never understood
those who barter bad for good.
How then all the waste construe
of loved ones sacrificed for you?
Why care if friends come fast or few
when all my friends I find in you?
Why search books and music through
If they ring falsely without you?

Oh, I would alter if I could
back to solitary good,
seal this split in what to do
to sever from, or fuse with you.
Illness, like a hangman's hood
quickens yearning to be good.
But I have entered earth anew
in radiant unison with you.

SLEEP

Release me from all conscious
thought,
from trouble and perplexity,
and with the peace that once I sought
let me dream;
And when I dream, unconsciously
may I still hear and think and see
and through the hours may I seem
to dream for an eternity.

DOUBTING

Dear heart, I dread to part with you
if only for a slender while
yet magnetise, through fantasies,
this horror to materialise.

And why? (Oh sweet, I love you so, too much, too much.)
Why? It is so that I,
perverse beyond belief,
seek to love you less, and wreak
the quarrels, sighs, complaints upon our love
instinctively
and hurt, be hurt the less, my love,
if ever we should part.

An envy of your erudition,
powers in knowledge, arts and charms,
then jealousy when others warm
within the radiance you cast,
and ever doubts of my own worth
and even doubts of you, your love.

Contentment in your company,
at best when calm felicity
inspires my heart,
at worst when superstitious spies
so deep a difference impart
that love assumes a gross disguise
and just upon a slight unease
can seem to blight the blessings that I prize.

A fibrous evil bites my heart
and cloaking round my reasoning
perpetrates the fate I fear.
I, serpent's gall and frail, so frail,
bring about the ruin of our joy.

I squander all to lessen pain,
to spite myself, to save myself, to fight against,
to bring about
the pain oh dearest heart the pain
that I need never know.

TYPES

You'd think, the way we ever look for
 better times ahead,
we weren't a race of pessimists
but optimists instead.
We're magnetising miracles
or wishing we were dead.

MAGICALLY COMPATIBLE

THE SPELL

Filled with high spirits,
 they tipped the seat.
There they sat, happily upside down,
the buts of mild jests
from passersby.

They swapped jokes,
clothes,
fags,
attitudes, tenderness,
mugs of chucked water.

He slaked her thirst,
fed her trash,
put her first,
spent his cash,
trudged the bus routes,
skipped meals,
shared his invective,
flair for fun.
Bright-edged where their outlines overlapped.
Magically compatible.

TRAINS

The god of travel has to be the train.
  Certainly for me.
That shared night bunk with my brother long ago,
racing to Capetown. And the green leather bolster
lost into the dark.

Then two proposals: on a stopped train in Venice
and on a country line to Brighton.
And meeting my beloved. A Frenchman?
The real thing now. And he was British all along.
Then the shared bunk on the Fat San
over to Kowloon,
a tight squeeze of ingenuity.

Dreams defined,
the thoughts, words and deeds fly past one's mind.
Yesterdays, now, and the tomorrows.

To be in charge of the beast,
controlling its brute speed!
To pull the slim passenger-packed serpent
swaying to a halt!

Yes, trains are in my line. Their rush and creak and hiss
are in my blood. Fill me with pride.
The kiss of life.

THE TRAIN

Rattling over sleepers,
shrieking past the field,
groaning under tunnels,
she sees the signals yield.

Nothing ever daunts her,
the great Torbay Express.
The pride of all the engineers
who bask in her success.

THE HERON

A hunched plump heron
on a tight green grassy mound,
feet touching a meter of
rapid running water
before the rough-and-tumble chaos
of the weir.
A pound for a sounding of its mood!

HEDGE SPARROWS

A threadbare hedge stuffed with cheeps,
each songbird eager to be heard,
and though one pauses, bends, and peeps
no clustered feathers, claws and beaks!
It is a conjuring trick most weird.
No bird seems there. All disappeared!

FAIRWHEEL

Lights.
The cold night air
and a reeling sky
and a blitz of stars
in flight,
while the wheel whirls bare
heaven and earth awry
up the path to Mars.
Bright
is the moon's white glare.
Someone's soulless cry.
Wild ecstatic fear.
Wild night.

SPRING

Since life began, each new mankind
has sung its praises to the spring
as though the past were deaf and blind
and suddenly they see and sing!
Bleak winter's rule has had its fling
and warming, wanes, and is resigned.

Each springtime we perceive anew
the leaves a-shimmer in the sun,
the grass fresh-mown or bright with dew,
till sight and scent fuse into one
and I dissolve in green and blue
and feel the pulse of growth begun.

I melt into the windless air
with birdsong purling in my ear,
I sense their flight from here to there
and see their song as jewels to wear
or loop about the garden sphere
where I lie, just half aware.

The happiness that summers bring
Is full and spacious as the days.
The harshnesses of winter sting
us into hyperactive ways.
But oh, the joy to live and praise
a world that once more gives us spring.

CONTRITION

Dearest, all my love is vain
when I think I've caused you pain.
Please forgive and please forget
now I own my wretched debt.

Please forgive, for of intent
to wound you, I was innocent.
Please forget that I could be
so short of sensitivity.

I cannot learn that you can't see
yourself the way you seem to me,
complete and perfect, far above
both mortal slight and mortal love.

May the pen which caused you pain
never, never write again,
for I should sooner die today
than drive our happiness away.

YOUNG TIGER

Dense fur,
sleekly stripey,
warmly tawny,
hiding the lithe sinews,
lying asleep.

Deep, infinitely deep,
throbbing, pulsing,
soft breath purring,
thrusting up through
the sluggish sloughs of
contentment,
worlds apart.

And a yawn –
a lazy display of a cave,
of a shell-pink cavern
with sifted, shelving,
rifted roof
and ice-white points of pearl.
A coral cave
of living flesh.

She slept again,
a rasping richness
blending in her breathing,
eyes looking inward,
green eyes,
glass eyes,
coolly luminous.

IN
HARNESS

THE GOOD LIFE

I loved animals once.
Now urine's welter sweeps the floors,
sprays the skirtings,
the cupboard doors.
Puppies trespass everywhere,
their mess everywhere,
ever renewed.
Feet tackled, no space traversed
without qualms, queasiness,
the stench of Dettol.

Cats victimised, flying
for surreptitious snacks
on dresser tops or windowsills,
while dogs watch wrathfully.
Cats on the bird-table
thumbing safe passages inside
and feathered life starves.
Scattered meat and meal,
papers and mucky bowls
lie rife. While outside
poultry leave their crusted
slops on paths and yard and cars
and every solid object in the barns.
Dog droppings too in straw and hay
and on the way to anywhere.

Ponies' tack and buckets dumped
along the hall, with boots galore,
grooming kit and gloves and hats
and mash-freckled torches. And a lamp.

No time for comfort, order, care,
no peace, no cash, no space to share.
Country, candle-wax and snow,
schools and faulty motors, vets.
And in my impotent despair
comes a new, prime dislike of pets.

THE BLACK CUILLIN

Looming, vapour-laden Cuillin,
sheep-cropped like tough suede,
pale green and Sauternes gold and Claret brown,
those round-skulled, dozing, moping pachyderms
beyond and still beyond,
soft-skinned in parts,
tight-runneled down their flanks.
Now mist gusts thickly through
their silent lair.
Did they move?
Or was it moving air?

WILD GEESE

In the field a feathered crop,
splay-footed, rooted in the stubble,
heads tilted on stalky necks'
stiff curves. Bead eyes interlinked
on lines of instinct's wing-power,
ready to break.
All-yielding, with flighty whim at one,
startled, they lift, plunder the air,
honk and clank their panic
in circular changes of mind.
They linger, drift and sink
their rough curtsy,
covering the field again in
fifty fat uprights.
Four laggard birds,
hypertensely slow,
land last. Then, laser-morse renewed,
they all graft again against the sky
and swim their dark shadows,
vacantly drilled to a microchip,
from sight.

MORE WILD GEESE

What I hear in my ears
is the rattle of a harrow,
the cheep of a phone,
the squeak of a barrow
and the scrape of a chain
on stone.

But the sight in my eyes
is a rill on the sand
and the spill of a wave
and the lift of the land
and the arch of a nave
and a bow strung loose
and an arrow which is
goose
            upon

                    goose

                            upon

                                goose

in impeccable flight.

COSMETICS

Cosmetics: and the young obsessed.
But nature knows best.
A shame to paint a youthful face.
There is no grace like natural grace
which, varnished, sickens without trace.

Those flunkies serving mother earth
hasten her raddled end,
ensuring us eternal dearth
of all organic grist and worth.

But girls, resist cosmetic power,
take global heed.
Suppose yourself a gilded flower,
a crop or pasture turning sour,
the soil eroding hour by hour,
a poisoned seed.

Let life-respecting sense devour
the phantom need.

EVOCATION

Painting word pictures of feelings.
Not an easy thing.
How to convey that loose-bowelled
sad pang, and drop of the heart?
Such innocent moments do it.
Nothing special, just poison-sweet,
unique to me, you, whoever.
Duping us back into a land of dreams.
Making us take another look at life.
Take stock of death.

DEATH

D eath is a fading into reality,
an excuse for the tired flesh
to crumble in the earth
and the spirit to be whirlwind blown
asunder
and whipped, stoned, blessed, enthroned.
Or, if of indeterminate worth,
sent spinning down through truth and space and snow
to have another go.
We think we know
about death.

ANONYMITIES

People are always hidden,
disguised inside their bodies,
filtering lies through their mouths
and eyes.
No-one knows what a soul is like,
cleverly disguised in its modest flesh
until death,
jigging the arms, the legs, the head
in shameful puppetry
until the flesh pulps
at its sudden limit and
the cunning, sly, never-known soul
flies out at last.
Stripped and lost and cold,
it flutters, crying 'Look, I'm free!
This is it, the actual living me!'
But no-one sees. They only
mourn the death,
their stubborn focus still upon the flesh.
So the soul flows into the empty air we breathe.
The conundrum is complete.
God's everlasting, fool-proof, wool-pulled
trick is conjured, while we
marvel, sigh, wipe our eyes and ask
'How is it done?'
And God replies,
'How can you be so blind?'

BIOGRAPHIES

People are best within books,
    released for the length of a read,
then shut back, reflected on,
resurrected in essence only,
each life a distinct taste,
savoury or sweet,
to roll around the palate of the mind,
acts and accents
relished in retrospect.

Shaped, pared, refined to a fine art,
shown wholly aesthetic as a laid-out corpse
at the last full-stop
of that first rehearsal run-through
in the flesh,
one holds the soul between covers.

Vast spaces spanned,
motions stirred
and fearful hopes evolved
in solid five-fold sense
while I, the weightless medium,
sit silent and invisible,
burning my own days
to feed their temple fires.
Why strive in here and now
with such galaxies of talent spent
in glorious bursts
before oblivion?

For even pages can't compress
the million witty words, oblique asides,
those anguished longings blessed or
mortified
all in vain
save for the embalming of the printer's ink
for the few.

I live vicariously
in biographers' editions
or, by courtesy of love,
most transient elixir of all,
in the rough draft of life.
Though most monumental
in subsequent editions
and in a reader's fertile mind.

RESOURCEFULNESS

The devil doesn't rest. His age-old quest
for wars of dedicated hatred and of gain
is seeking now the brightest and the best
in cyber's dark domain
to spotlight victims, innocent or vain.
To spread the world with poison east to west,
from north to south. The internet infest
with terror and with pain.

GOD OF LOVE

Oh God of love who wrought the snow
to blight the spring buds as they grow,
and rob the grazing beasts of grass
and make of life a dismal farce,

that God who improvised the rain
which falling, floods the Third World grain
and falling not, still brings about
that equal persecution, drought.

Earthquake, storm, disease - these all
contribute to man's random thrall.
Yet, darlings of his universe,
we may be violent and perverse
to ease our suffering and exploit
all soulless creatures less adroit
at godlike impudence. But still
most animals can kill at will
within their predatory scope,
so therein lies their grounds for hope.

This world is based on pain and fear,
brief joy is neither there nor here
it is so transient. But lo,
He loves us all the same, we know,
and specially those who suffer most
and never of contentment boast.

And if, with paltry human love
we feel protected from above
how swiftly does our God react
and jealously destroy the fact.
And would we once love out of turn
it's down to hell and there to burn.

SAINT JOHN'S FIRE

The celebration for Saint John
came too soon,
from outer darkness
before the solstice
before the dawn
bursting up from nowhere,
breaking rules of safety,
flouting humanity in sheets of fire
sky high
on moor, through forest,
ripping down the coast
like no tomorrow.
No anti-inflammatory yarrow
or healing plants
to pacify
our urgent prayers.

A BIRTHDAY

My day of birth.
The ticking clock, the turning wheel,
a sense of being tricked to fill the role
of one year older.
Oddly, all I feel
is neither old nor wise, but only new,
reborn this Easter day to weigh the world
and wonder what is true.

An Easter birthday and a fear that all
the great Creation and the fatal Fall
are part and parcel of a rigid plan,
and Christ a well-primed pawn who had to die,
with minor destinies for every man
mapped out, plus snakes and traitors of their own.
Intelligence programmed stage by stage
as decades mount towards catastrophe
with arbitrary wage of good or ill
while here we live, allotted by the Will
we call religion
till men create the new oblivion.

My day of birth, bright Easter morn,
once more reborn the awful certainty
that I've still failed as wife and mother too,
as writer and in all things left or done
or felt or thought since that first breath I drew
switched my clock on.

TODAY THE DEVIL CAME TO ME

Today the devil came to me
and merged his horny skin with mine
till, like a canker in a tree
he filled each crevice, fold and line.

He pressed so close against my heart
it shrank, recoiling, dulled and numb
to those who hitherto no art
could fetter to some rule of thumb.

Husband, daughters, little son,
wither in my double stare;
the devil kindling me to shun
their innocent desire to share.

Vampire clamped within my frame
he sucks the blood of tenderness,
injecting back the self-fired flame
that lusty egos must possess.

The devil came because he read
the stark resentment in my face,
like a wolf whose ego fed
upon the children's fall from grace.

Motherhood has squandered youth
but rancour is the devil's kiss,
for sour strikes sweet upon his tooth
and tempts me to a dark abyss.

FICTION

The habit of fiction dies hard.
Magpie twists of tinsel
littering the brain,
a mad distraction.
While bits of tat remain,
reality shies away,
things unseen,
facts dropped. Forgotten
the story-lines
like tangled threads of yarn
spread untellable.
Why this urge to create
episodes of other lives
with here and now in shadow?
This neglect of friends,
the impulse to evade,
then, letting go,
a bruising sense of loss.
Cruel compulsion.
Sad, the senseless shunning,
the bitter mourning,
that cannot make amends

DEPESSION

Like poison in the veins, depression crawls.
She suffocates my smiles with fingers chill,
gloating, she nurses me with curdled milk
to feed this sick and melancholy will.

Yes, sick and weak indeed, I have succumbed
to cloying sweetness, burdening the flesh,
affording fleeting pleasure, soon displaced
by rancid self-despair and bitterness.

And still depression sinks her weary weight
till pricks of self-reproach for work undone
cramp all my limbs, numb as these routine days,
stagnant between the reign of moon and sun.

THE SERVICE

The room is still
as one shuttered.
Sunlight flutters in the close-focus tree, liquid bright.
Painted scrolls whirl slowly
in lilac and rose
over the great panes
like emblems of the soul.

There is no air, only a holy void
and the frail compost of
perpetual incense swung.
The walls are shadow mauve.
I sit,
a question mark fading into space.
Tight blunt doubts
unfurl like paper buds floated.
I am a maths problem solved
or Greek translated.
I weigh death as a slice of life,
hollow with good intentions.

Sharp qualms melting as wax
into soft consents,
I face the moment of truth,
the box of my mind
laid X-ray bare.

The censer snarls at my sickness of sin.
My suppliant eyes receive
Christ's image, the altar, and the architrave in colour;
but shut, the tableau point blank
is branded white and grey,
with Christ in black.

IN HARNESS

When life is threatened with disease
our timeless longings seem to freeze,
and 'now' becomes a constant taste
of bitter-sweet impending waste.
The will's first buck of disbelief
abruptly knuckles down its grief
into a steady harnessed pace
with mind and body face by face
and while they keep the same direction
life wheels by with smooth deception,
bearing-reins with cruel guile
presenting the correct profile.

But phantoms catch us unawares.
Just let the leader of the pair
once shy or falter, willpower wanes
and brute confusion takes the reins.
There's no stampede, no ugly scene,
but withered hopes hang down between
the horse of thought, the horse of limb,
till life, while precious, smoulders dim,
a worthless prize. Then angels come
and with miraculous aplomb
take steeds in hand and trim the cart
with steel to will and joy to heart
and in their glorious enterprise
drive firmly forth beneath the skies.

FOUR
CHILDREN

BEATRICE

I was born in Bangkok, and then went to Laos,
and a home up on poles was my very first house.
There were temples with bells and strange symbols so old
and the women wove silk and wore silver and gold.
There were buffalo ploughing and thin river ships
and the children held children like toys on their hips.
There were parasols, flowers, and dances serene,
One Million Elephants, a King and a Queen.

I then lived in London, in grey city air,
in a flat at the top of a house on a square.
This square had a garden with grass and some trees
and a few stony paths which were hard on the knees.
Some elderly ladies might potter about
but seldom, oh seldom, a child came out.

When I was just four on a cold April morn
life turned upsidedown when my sister was born.
We moved across London and this time the square
had a church in the middle and friends living near.
My bedroom was little and crooked and high
at the top of the house, with a view of the sky.
We had a back garden within a brick wall
with roses, an ash tree and grass over all.
In this house my sister was so free from care
that she rode on her tricycle right down the stair.

We then bought a house with the forest all round
where foxes and badgers and deer could be found.
A farmer nearby kept horses and cows
and our lives were as free as school-time allowed.
We walked with our dogs and we climbed all the trees,
we swung upon ropes and we played as we pleased.
We now have a sister of two, which is fun,
and a poor baby brother who's still only one.

BECCY

Dramatic birth at home. The ambulance.
But what a baby triumphed back to base!
The broken toddler nights, the imperious will,
the laughing blue-eyed Botticelli face.

A watcher from the side at play and school,
those eyes missed nothing, while the fair-haired head
stood slightly taller than her peers. Alone,
imagination sharpening her dread.

A small girl at the piano, confident,
inventing her own music, her own roles
of doctors, pupils, heads of mythic schools,
lit from within, warming older souls.

Teachers, classmates, boyfriends, pills,
a roller coaster from the shy to wild,
this wholesome and explosive adult girl
kept all the fun and talents of the child.

ROMOLA

She lies asleep,
her bedroom nest feathered
with watching angels,
not in rigid vigilance
but pensive and pliant,
their wings weave
a wreath about her bed.
Their pulse of love
sustains her in her quest.

Nightly we trespass
the widths of space
and depths of time
without the body's bounds,
like hounds unleashed
then called, at dawn, to heel.
We tread the tethered, tired, terrestrial round
in wakeful day with dwindling zeal
till night sleeps slice us free
to pioneer the bright abyss anew.

But this small child,
how wholesomely she comes and goes
from solid day
to transcendental night,
the world of matter yielding to her play
in seamless flow
until her force of life
burns low, and back
to actual being she must go,
where dreams are mirror images of truth.

ROLLO

I remember how we waved him away.
The car packed up, stocked, roped,
went slowly up the drive
between the cherry trees.

So many times he'd shot off behind the wheel
on pleasure bent - for work - some enterprise.

This time was special –
full of heart, hope for happiness,
the moment crystalised.

He rang later, still short of London.
He'd had a speeding fine. Still of good cheer.

So much life unfurled since.
Marriage. A child. At heart a Londoner.

THE
SENIOR
CITIZEN

MATURITY

'I don't need to go to school again,' she says.
  'I know everything.'
She is four.
Queues, order, songs to sing,
lessons like a jolly box of colours.
All no more.

I understand. I peaked at four.
That sunny confidence.
Now the sting.

BOOKS AS FRIENDS

We read a book second time
and find it changed, for we have changed.
We loved it then, now it's still fine,
though all the text seems rearranged.

We learn new people as with books.
Their sense can shift by hour, by page.
Assessing text and tone and looks,
we learn their essence stage by stage.

ON DAVID'S 80TH BIRTHDAY

Four score years, and never better!
Time for poetry and praise!
Doggrel? That won't upset him
on this joyful day of days.
Master of the written word,
the spoken word and yes, IT,
no-one more fun, more quite absurd.
Friends with many great and good
in Scotland, England, far and wide,
he tells of bad Glen Bogle's storms
across the Scottish countryside.
He's Master Chef above all cooks,
fantastic dishes all his own,
he's written, and he's published books
but muddles up his mobile phone.
Where rude Glen Bogle breaks trees down
our hero's planted hundreds more,
a landscape genius like Brown
he fills our hearts with abject awe.
His children represent his arts,
they echo him in different ways.
He is a man of many parts
who never ceases to amaze.

DIAMOND WEDDING

Sixty years shared, two souls combine,
your brilliant mind and face still mine.
Good humour. Unperturbed. A sun
that shaped our space
with intricate design.
My heart's companion, fiction read, and spun.
Your printing press begun.

Met at fate's whim as happens ever,
though perfect fits, a miracle too clever –
at odds on climate, health, and food.
And food for health.

Across these years your youthful spirits cheer
as at the start, when quoting Belloc, Lear,
we doubled into taxis bound
for Restoration romps, French farce,
freeing inhibitions bang on cue,
expressing selves as selves we scarcely knew.

Best friends, until on whim those fates intend
the years beyond these sixty reach their end.

OLD AGE

Who says age is like a ripened fruit?
I say it is a blight,
a souring, slowing, grumbling knowingness,
a struggling to live long.
It hasn't quite the healthiness of death
which, after all, is right.
It only bears the illnesses of life
gone irreparably wrong.

THE DOOMED SHOPPING EXPEDITION

Full of good will. Full of good cheer.
Here to buy food. There to fetch her.
A wonderful juggling with spirits of joy.

Then discordant descanting disputes that destroy.
Cross-hatchings of purpose, crossed lines in the mind,
a fraught hour of muddle that neither designed.

FALLING

Feet skimmed the ground,
mind fixed on ticking tasks
one by one.
Time of the essence.

As a bolt from below
a toe blocked, like a brake.
The long, mesmerising hurtle
and the smash.

Stunned, grazed, skinned,
one trip the wiser.
List of must-haves lost …
but skeletally sound.

LEADERS

A crude boy with cash and clout
wins the day
with cheap and cheerful ease.

Scorns to appease,
lets logic, fact and commonsense
hold sway his way.

Another boy with clout:
Kim Jong-un swaps jibes with Uncle Sam.
Two nurseries tricked out
with deadly toys and tools.
Tomfoolery rules.

Egypt's brutal Sisi,
Syria's lisping, blue-eyed pest,
pale Putin's scrutinising gaze towards the West …
all round the globe, a cast of bullies
on a gimcrack stage,
a pop-up army each, a fur-lined robe
and self-promoting rage.

RECESSION

Friday the thirteenth, the world has gone bust,
along with their promises, hopes and our trust.
Squandering virtual money away
turns day into night and work into play.

The dominoes topple, the viruses spread,
The figures go spiraling into the red.
They're juggling the noughts as with bubbles of soap.
Are they crazy on crack or dreaming on dope?

The world works in cycles on scales to deplore.
They'll conquer this monster. We've been here before.

BREXIT

Absurd small state with monumental past,
quirky, modest, reticent, sublime.
Uncertain now, and fractured, and out-classed.
We're out of step, of partners and of time.
Give Britannia a hand for ruling the waves ...
your loyal approval is all that she craves.

PANDEMIC NOW

Not many things I'd give the world for.
Who would want a world so sick?
God who made it? Any God?
They all have washed their hands of it.

PRAYERS

Sadly now, our chapel's out of bounds.
No Sunday gathering.
We fear pandemic virus on the wing,
explained by science,
not in the heart.
Our faith would not be worth
a pinch of salt
if this impurity outweighed integrity
right from the start.
The priest celebrates alone.
We have his sermon only on our screens,
sanitised, apart.
Our candle flickers here.
The gentle drift of spirits in the incense
over there.

LOCKDOWN

All locked down from life we know,
families, couples, or alone.
Dressed up or down, nowhere to go.
Missing pleasures all our own.
Coffee stops. Cafes galore.
Galleries loved, or to explore,
and flights to everywhere.
No more. We've shot our bolt.
We've gone too far.
Our world is wracked with wear and tear
from plane and car.
Time to halt. Draw breath. Search soul.
Time for nature to revolt
from pole to pole.
What's the betting, free again,
we'll head for Europe, the Far East,
the United States? Life is insane
until economies fail.

"Essential funding must increase!"
We chafe and fret
in lockdown sweat
for faith, or science, to find a voice.

VACCINATIONS

One day, perhaps not soon,
our scientists will say
'Today we're clear.
Farewell to gloom. To fear.
Love is in the air!'
Pandemic strictures will be banned,
masked faces, sterile hands,
unsociable spacing.
Meanwhile schools, pubs, shops,
businesses, banks
break down. Give up. Run dry.
Then waves of sickness hit us from afar,
death numbers climb as in the blinking of an eye.
Strive on into another start,
shutters up and cheerful awnings taut.
We baited bears once upon a time.
Now Covid has its sport.

PIGEON WISDOM

What do pigeons always say?
Human fancy runs away
but in this lockdown, clear as day,
'Let's all beat Covid', croons away.
'Let's all beat Covid', day by day,

'Let's all beat …'
Pause.
Ad nauseam.

BRENDA

She was a bit of a rebel.
That was nice.
Spoke with a slow drawl. Posh
but democratic.
She liked odd-bods with dogs,
poked fun at us flat owners
who walked with sticks, and things on wheels.
Old fogies.
She was seventy-eight.
Her home smart and charming,
her garden stuffed with roses, and a doocot.
Post-Covid we hoped to ask her here
to swap some gossip.
Cancer hit her while she still looked good.
Removals came today. Her choice belongings
going into store.

GILDING LILIES

Handsome and historic and nearby
stands beautiful St Mary's. The bare-faced
walls ascending, moonlight lit.
Stone blocks, grey and umber-pink, stacked high
with reticent magnificence.

In the evening now
a rosy-tinted glow clings to each wall
like colour filtering from a sunset sky
but flooded from two earth-bound lamps
and shading sickly green into the turf.

With light pollution rife, why waste expense
where vivid crocus bulbs await their birth?

THE TEAPOT

Spun glass fragile, transparent clarity,
a hint of heat-resistant modernity,
a finely balanced duck
quaffing quarts of boiling water
without a qualm. No alarm.
Despite our carefulness and calm
an object struck her from above.
Her spout imploded
with a flustered charm.

THE CUP

Washing his precious cup
with bated breath
I clipped it smartly on the rim
against a tap.
My heart shrank in.
My stomach looped the loop.
I stooped and picked the pieces up.
Come, welcome death!

HER
MOTHER'S
DAUGHTER

MAMA

Oh Mother dearest, ever more I miss
your heart and mind.
Tranquil. Confiding that and this.
Our souls combined
to touch the raw, or see the funny side,
re-visit people shared
with pain, or pride,
with freshness unimpaired by time
and all perceived through you,
world-wise, inspiriting life-guide.

If we could only be together
growing old, challenges compared,
gaining aches, victims of the weather,
losing balance, losing confidence,
loss of memory feared.

Laid out between us, just a game
of overcoming: still being Constance.

HOW HAVE I FAILED YOU?
LET ME COUNT THE WAYS

Flight to another world, an Eastern dream.
Land of the Million Elephants and the White Parasol
but you not there
and I a mummy's girl.
Not parted in the heart, still part of you
but dumbed by love elsewhere.
Not instantly in touch, feeding news to you.
Our Wedding Day,
Embassy guests, new friends.
No you.
Home leave with your first grandchild
to my aunt's big house in Hove,
not the little Coach House with you.
Your drive to London blanketed in snow,
your wait there, like a guest. Child two is born
in the next room. Second place again.
Then Tim's attacks,
critical and cruel on his childhood past,
a heaven which in another mood he wished could last.
I should have praised my brother's wit and skill
not censured him.
You stayed with us and broke your hip.
I long to turn that clock back so I sit
hour by hour with you in hospital,
your daughter in the ward.
Those precious meals with you in your flat
when I was dull,
not sharing more child memories of Hove.
Questions unasked that still give pain.
And did I speak to family, or friends,
as if you were not there?

I was with you in your flat
when Tim explained your move to "care".
And then I left.
I visited you there,
staying with Tim.
Not long each time.
Too constrained by him.
And, sin of sins, to be away
when you were frail and moving on.
Not holding you, dear one, when you had gone.

TIM

DEAR TIM

My elder brother. We shared a world:
Egypt, Natal, Lincolnshire. Childhood unfurled
where our father was a child.
Fine house, garden, riding in the wood.
Father's war was tough. We lost him for good.
He took another wife.
Tim shut that out. He never understood.

In Sussex Tim grew less kind.
Stayed spellbound
by early years. A perfect climate, peace profound.
His child's happiness in heart and mind.

He had four children. So did we. All eight
met through their lives, despite the fate
of distance, and Tim's dark dictate.
Those meetings funny, nervy, lie behind.

So strange, so quirky, failing in the round.
So tender now and then. So sometimes good.
A captive child into manhood hurled,
now dying. Thoughts of wide success too late.

His talent, humour, aims. All gone to ground.
Childhood still bright. His day is night. And he is blind.

TIM

In Durban Tim escaped from school,
hiding his tie. He was no fool.
To Mooi River then we went,
the happiest year Tim ever spent,
finding snakes and riding bikes
and burning grasses in the dykes.
He ever mourned a span too short
at boys school, where Aunt Phyllis taught.
He liked to ride at the polo ground
reporting at a canter where potholes were found.
The voyage home was very risky,
vast waves in the Bay of Biscay.
Albany Villas was our home
when we were off the Drottningholm.
Our Mother took, without her spouse,
the other grandparental house
and five good years Tim then spent there,
cycling about in Lincolnshire.
To prep school he was then propelled
where he immediately excelled,
became a first class rifle shot
and in athletics beat the lot.
At Uppingham he was House Head,
experienced gliding's thrilling dread,
shot at Bisley. Training course –
Officer in the Royal Air Force.
Met his Margaret. Married her.
Lived in North London year by year.
The children came, two girls, two boys.
His darling, sweet-heart, real life toys.
He ever after lived in Hove
from where he simply would not move.

INTOLERANCE

Being fully adult seems to me
to bring the worst out in humanity.
My brother's years at university
have made him critical to a degree.

We both know, oh too well, frustrated gloom,
the foolishness and ugliness that bloom,
but worms of criticism eat his heart
and place him in a soured world apart.
His sense and sensibility in art
give little satisfaction or support.

Can the critical, with mind acutely styled,
and the tolerant, with heart, be reconciled?

MEN

JIGSAW MAN

Behold! a figure of elan -
a jigsaw man, a puzzle man.
Each piece in situ. I could hit you,
twice-split image, twice-cracked sham!

Be of good heart, take him apart,
explore his hollow mystery.
Then, negative and ghostly, can
you learn the subtle shadow man.

THE VISIT

War over, this father paid a visit to his childhood house.
His wife lived there. 'This is for you!'
A Bentley, purely masculine, brutish elegance
snarling on the gravel under the yew,
perfect for a crowded market town.
'Of course you'll have to master her.'
A tense sadistic day, spun like brittle glass,
wife in purgatory at the wheel,
the children passionately partisan behind,
martyrs trampled by the dog.

'I'll build a garden wall,' he said, 'and Timothy can help.'
And Timothy can help with gritted teeth,
regretting the pear tree's hammock,
the greengage tree and the field,
his life of harem peace.
No pleasant interlude with ponies
in their multi-scented paddocks,
wasps in jars, trollies on the lawn.

An indoor shattering of cups, an angry roar.
'The child only slipped, she missed the step.'
'Your nails are bitten.'
Shoes not clean.
A magic pause in bed; and Doctor Doolittle read -
the jolly doctor in her father's stead.
Their love of animals shared,
his charm distinctly felt - but swiftly gone.

A Christmas card from London, the present of a tie!
His wife may notice by all means
and ache to thaw his love.
He speaks not a word,
the pouting bully, obdurately mute.
The musical box still plays as when he was a boy,
his mother's home is still intact.
Grimly smug to see his theory proved,
he went that day, with Christmas only yesterday.
They had no need for him.
No punishment deserved. No favour given.
A wife who could not cope with sporting gears.

In her London flat his mistress heard,
'Constance put not one foot wrong.
She even brought me Ovaltine in bed!'
And in her mirage paradise his wife
sat behind the wheel, applied her heel,
engaged the double clutch and, will of steel,
jolted down the drive to live her life.

INCONSISTENCY

When men dispute and countries are at war
a bestial hatred dominates the soul,
weak love is pinioned by an eagle claw
and misery is left to take its toll.

And when a soldier, fed with battle psalms,
destroys his foes with calculated zest,
the frenzied nation opens wide its arms
and pins another medal to his chest.

Yet when in peace this man commits a crime,
and all cry out against his villainy,
and with one voice condemn him in his prime,
does God approve our inconsistency?

ASPIRATIONS

We're fit to mould these perfect males
in womb, and down long childhood trails,
and even offer bread and wine
provided neither is divine.
But there's the rub. As adult souls
the meek and gentle have no roles.
We're raped and murdered every day,
yet man it is who walks God's way;
who does not scruple to observe
that women are not fit to serve.

With mind and body incomplete
as Eve, still branded with deceit
(a put-up job from first to last:
God wrote the plot and chose the cast)
we're symbols both of love and sex
and vapid faith. But must not vex
the clergy with a plea for space
in which to manifest God's Grace.

Religion is a club, and we
the trivia who make the tea.
The moral's plain: to be let in
we need the force of greed and sin
for in provoking fear and dread
our brothers are light years ahead,
and going to meet our heavenly fates
we'll find them picketing the gates.

EARLY AND OCCASIONAL PIECES

THE SEA

There lay the grey-green winter sea
  and, as an angry lion roars,
it roared and, prowling on its shores,
spat foam and spray repeatedly.
The sky was dark and full of rain
which fell, and ceased, and fell again.

The months passed by: May, June, July.
There lay the sea, a summer sea,
which carried ships contentedly
and rocked them with a sober sigh.
The sky was blue, unflushed by rain.
The sea was equable again.

BRIGHTON AND HOVE

I love Brighton, going back years;
embracing the Downs from the train,
Jack and Jill perched high, waving chattily
their mill sails to the chalky sprawl,
the suburbs and the sea.
Criss-cross below the trains
cheap streets of barrow bargains
run up to Prinny's gardens –
his pavilion's exotic face,
dotty onion domes against the sky.
Brighton. Its Regency swagger and its grace.
And here Old Steine spreads her apron out
with stately space, then crescents grandly railed.
Saint Peter's Church.
Memories of breakfast with Mabs
before days at college studying art.
Walking from the station, Queen's Street blocked
by the Clock Tower. And lower, on the right
people search for bargains in the Lanes.
The throngs on Palace Pier.
West Pier was set on fire, routinely mocked,
washed up. Mother as a girl swam the bright
summer stretch between the two.
Facing on the Front, now long lost,
stood Mutton's Restaurant for the wealthy few:
striped awnings, swank and plush,
the speciality turtles tanked and doomed within the door.
Thackeray came for soup.
Outside, the passing piquant seaside crush,
with Mother gazing upwards at a thrush,
along to gentle Hove. The properties
bought by my grandparents for rent.
Their own house Regency,
with long back garden

and fine fig tree in front.
Fuller's white-iced walnut cake for tea,
their sugar-dusted butterballs to suck.
George Street, shops of every sort.
Not Continental then. When did it start:
boxed trees, shiny tables, coffee shops?
Hove and Brighton. Generations.
Grandparents. Aunt. My brother's family.
Our children.
More and more memories,
Phyllis, Jack -
and Mother at the heart.

40 ALBANY

Albany Villas in Hove - 40 Albany.
Just 40.
Granny and Grandpa Parsons at the start.
We slept in the jam tarts room,
nine ornate flowers along the cornice.
Grandpa with his stick to 'beat us goodnight',
his painted tins for charity, red blue and green
on used newspaper.
Grandpa on the well-railed veranda
'taming birds to the finger.'
The picture of a group below a castle:
his trick of 'Someone's waving!'
and our looking just too late.

Granny's rough shifts,
thick elastic round the top,
for struggling out of costumes
after swims.
Rugs, towels and a Lilo spread on pebbles
and baskets packed with tea.

The Regency drawing room
with big bay window, velvet hung.
Modern brickwork fireplace,
chintzy three-piece-suite.
The little stairs below a window:
one turn of carpet-worn creaks
then down to rooms below the garden.

The reign of Aunty Phyllis and Uncle Jack.
The Civic Trust. Their strong support.
Aunty's aromatic fruit cakes in the kitchen
and aproned Winnie smiling by the sink.
Jack watching cricket at the county ground.
Meals without number down the long table,
all us young ones visiting.
The roast potatoes! White and gold meringues!

IMPRINTS FROM CHILDHOOD

Two children on an upper deck saw hills of water rise,
which climbed on every side it seemed, and blotted out the skie
The little ship, the Drottningholm, would wallow in the rough
then struggle slowly upwards, to be plunged back in the trough.
The helmsman was in panic when he realised their plight,
leaving the ship to pitch and roll as he collapsed in fright.

An Anglican was leading an indomitable crowd
all challenged to keep standing and keep singing strong and loud.
They sang for their salvation in their peril on the sea
while wind and wave raved on in fierce indifference to their plea.

A gentle waft of oranges was hanging in the air
remembered by the children as an antidote to fear.
There was chaos in the hair salon from an escaping chair
with bottles smashing, shampoo gushing, bubbles everywhere.

The children crouched and sent their metal Dinkies down the deck
They ate where other stomachs failed, as crockery lay in wrecks.
Calm waiters bore their trays to those still ready for their food.
The seats were clamped, the soup was off, the table manners rude

The Bay of Biscay lay behind. The sun smiled from the sky.
At Cape Verde, calm at anchor, stacked bananas swung up high
and boys dived for the pennies flung them from the liner's rails,
a sight of mutual delight that lightened past travails.

Sports: with floating apples to be grabbed just by the face.
One child at last defeated and ashamed of her disgrace.
A window pane set on a deck revealing far below
young dancers doing Tap, their neat feet knocking in a row.

Another peaceful day on deck, when someone coolly said,
'Is that a mine? It's floating near, perhaps we'll soon be dead!'
A move towards the railings, as to watch a buoy float near,
and the mine bobbed gently closer, even closer … and was clear!

One passenger, whose wife had boarded ship while very ill,
asked the children to their cabin where they both sat very still.
She gave them each a present, one an ivory rabbit white.
She quietly passed away as England slowly came in sight.

POSTSCRIPT

These poems contain so many personal references that a biographical note may be helpful.

Philippa was born in Alexandria on 22 April, 1939. Her father, John Bunting, was a newly commissioned Captain in the Royal Army Medical Corps. Seeing war coming, he had volunteered immediately after qualifying. Her mother, Constance Parsons, was four years older than her husband. She was a dashing and highly organised young woman, indestructibly photogenic. She had auditioned for the screen before her marriage, to realise instantly that the tedium of film was not for her.

At the time of Philippa's birth the world was still peaceful enough for Constance's unmarried sister Phyllis to join them from England. Her role was to help with Philippa and her brother Tim, then an enterprising toddler of two. Within six months war had been declared. Everyone was stuck. Astonishingly, this did not prevent Constance from organising a holiday in Cyprus the following year. Philippa took her first steps in the Trudos Mountains, in the grounds of the famous but eerily empty Hotel Berangaria. While they were there, Italy entered the war. Next year, with the rapid advance on Egypt of the Afrika Korps, civilian dependents were evacuated. Constance, Phyllis and the children were settled temporarily in Durban. Within a year they moved to Mooi River, where there was a boys' school for Tim. In his own imagination, it set standards of happiness which no other school was ever to match.

As soon as the war was over the evacuees were repatriated, an adventurous experience recorded in the early "Imprints from Childhood." After a temporary stay in Hove with her parents, Constance moved to John's boyhood home in Lincolnshire - but without John, who remained on active service. He never lived permanently with the family again.

As was usual in professional classes at the time, the children were quickly dispatched to boarding schools. Tim went immediately, first to his father's prep school in Eastbourne, then to his father's public school (Uppingham) and eventually to Peterhouse, his father's college in Cambridge.

Philippa's departure was less draconian. She enjoyed a happy year in the local school before being sent to Moira House, also in Eastbourne, where she was miserably homesick. The possibility of enrolling her in the local grammar school was never considered.

The theoretical benefits, if any, of having Philippa and her brother in Eastbourne seem not to have materialised. The only advantage was the proximity of Aunt Phyllis in Hove, and even that was not much use. She rescued Philippa when she was quarantining after mumps. Apart from that, contact was not encouraged.

Philippa went to Brighton Arts College after leaving school, only to be whisked away to finishing school in Paris before she could graduate. Secretarial work followed, first in Brighton, at a solicitor's office, then in London, with the then well known film company, ABPC. Many of these adventures are recorded in her novels. Her writing is strongly autobiographical, although Philippa denies it. She has always believed that to describe a character to the life and then disguise him or her with a moustache makes identification impossible.

I picked Philippa up on a train soon after joining HM Diplomatic Service. Or she picked me up, depending on who is telling the story. Our marriage in Laos is an example of her courage and loyalty. Shortly after our engagement the Foreign Office posted me to Vientiane, where there had been a coup. I was told that conditions were so dangerous that travel by dependents could not be authorised. On arrival I was surprised to find dependents firmly entrenched. This prompted me to ask the Ambassador if the presumption against Philippa's joining me was as strong as I had been told. Not at all, he assured me: he preferred his staff to be married and accompanied. Philippa was with me within a month, undeterred by a military countercoup, including a hand-to-hand battle in the streets of Vientiane. We were married on 19 January, 1961, at HM Embassy.

Although Vientiane was theoretically a "hardship" post, we had three of the best years of our life there. The highpoint was the birth of Beatrice in 1962.

After Vientiane we had three years in London, where Beccy

was born. We then discovered Rudolf Steiner and moved to Sussex, to be near Michael Hall School. In 1973 a brilliantly happy posting to Berlin followed, where Romola and Rollo were born in the British Military Hospital.

After a further short period in London I transferred to the Scottish Office. We bought a dilapidated property in Midlothian and settled into the routine described in "The Good Life." When, after three decades, we decided to buy a more manageable house in Haddington, the children deployed every argument they could to prevent the move - even though they had all left home by now. What they thought was their most telling point was that the dogs would never settle for town life. In the event the dogs were never happier. The same proved true for us.

The streak of melancholy woven through some of Philippa's poems - "A Birthday" for example, or "Fiction" or "Depression" - may well have its roots in her parents' divorce. Constance did everything she could to save the marriage, and everything she could to preserve good relations between John and the children. Her strategy was to explain the rift in terms of the stress John had suffered, leading, she claimed, to a mental breakdown. This does not tally with John's account. According to him, he had a "good" war. He certainly saw his fair share of action, and was decorated for it: Tobruk, the Western Desert, Greece, India and, finally, Burma, where he commanded a medical unit at Kohima. There may have been a mental crisis later, when he was re-establishing medical services in the Federated Malay States. But the marriage was in trouble well before then.

Constance's determination not to let the children catch a hint of hurt or bitterness made matters worse. Both of them picked up unerringly on her real feelings. Tim resolved the problem by refusing to see his father at all if he could possibly avoid it. Philippa did her best to follow Constance's wishes. She saw her father regularly and came, eventually, to feel a troubled affection for him.

Be that as it may, her resentment against John emerges in poems such as "The Visit." Tim gets it in the neck in her youthful "Intolerance" - and I dread to think where her excoriating "Jigsaw Man" comes from. Even "Aspirations" can hardly be read as what it seems to be, an attack on Christianity. The Christian Community, which we attend, has had women priests and bishops for years. To put it mildly, men get a mixed press where Philippa is concerned.

The odd thing is that Philippa and I both found it easy to talk with her parents. We regret now that we did not ask some of the questions which only occurred to us when it was too late. I would bet that some of her admirers, reading these poems, will feel the same about Philippa.

A few further notes.

Philippa started to collect her poetry when she was eight. The earliest in this collection is "The Train," written when she was ten, and inspired by a card game she used to play with Tim. "Sleep," in the Existential Angst Section, was written when she was sixteen, as was "The Sea," in the last Section (Early and Occasional Pieces). Her closing poem, the evocation of childhood trauma in "Imprints from Childhood," is more recent. Other examples of her teenage poetry will no doubt be easily recognisable, mainly in the opening two Sections. Although derivative in some cases, even her earliest work contains flashes of the originality and wit which mark her poetry as a whole.

Philippa's later poems involve the difficulty that very few are dated. It has been easy enough, in most cases, to establish text and general context, but not always an exact order. The present arrangement attempts to provide a reliable idea of her artistic development (covering some seventy years), while highlighting the themes she addresses with such honesty.

Editing has encountered a number of problems. Her early poems are characterised by a proliferation of colons, semicolons, dots and dashes. Many of her later ones contain little punctuation at all. An early and misguided attempt on my part to impose some sort of consistency has achieved a reduction in the number of semicolons in a few of the poems. That's about it. In the end I realised that the only sensible policy was to leave well alone.

Of the individual sections, it would be a mistake to assume

that all the poems in the Existential Angst Section relate to the same man. Phiippa was a knock-out, with many suitors, a situation which has continued for years. In the Magically Compatible Section, "Fairwheel" and "Young Tiger" are among her early poems. "Young Tiger" is about the family tabby, a forerunner of the cats appearing in "The Good Life."

The In Harness Section is more diversified, a reflection of the ups and downs of family life. There are some regrettable lacunae. Our most memorable cat, the infamous Mrs Bauldron, does not appear. Nor does Mrs Bauldron's fellow criminal, our pug dog, Horace. "Saint John's Fire" evokes the pagan celebration of midsummer, its Christian counterpart, and the alarming evidence then coming to light about climate change. Philippa spotted this early. "In Harness" itself, which gives the Section its name, was prompted by her remission from breast cancer. Here, as in a number of her poems, the particular seems to stand for something more complex and introspective.

The Senior Citizen Section includes a few of Phiippa's short, ephemeral outbursts. These are probably best read, not as definitive pronouncements on current affairs, but as examples of the frustrations of growing old. Her poems about accidental breakages reinforce the theme in a more light-hearted way.

In the Occasional Pieces Section, note how, in "Imprints from Childhood," memory plays its usual tricks. The SS Drottningholm must have reached the Cape Verde Islands before, not after, the storm in the Bay of Biscay. Philippa remembers it the other way round, so that is how it is recorded. Her unverifiable account of the panicking helmsman ought perhaps to be taken with a pinch of salt, even if it is so deeply felt that it subverts the discipline of her youthful, four-line stanzas.

The Drottningholm, incidentally, was a small passenger liner, launched on the Clyde in 1909 as the RMS Virginian. During the Second World War, painted white and on charter to the neutral Swedes, she was used for the exchange of prisoners of war. She was still in her bright, war-time livery when Philippa travelled on her. Although technically advanced for her time, the design of her hull seems to have been suboptimal. Her tendency to pitch and toss earned her the sobriquet of the Rollingholme.

This may help to explain, if not wholly validate, the myth of the terrified helmsman.

The connection with Sussex celebrated in some of Philippa's Occasional Pieces is part-homage, part-boast about the status of her mother's family. Through the de Moutons they trace back to the Norman Conquest. Perhaps the brio of these simple ballads will help revive the family's pride in its imperfectly documented history.

October, 2021

INDEX OF FIRST LINES

Lightning Source UK Ltd.
Milton Keynes UK
UKHW010847101121
393713UK00001B/8